MY BABY JOURNAL

Based on

Dirty Wow Wow and Other Love Stories

by CHERYL and JEFFREY KATZ

Photographs by HORNICK/RIVLIN

TEN SPEED PRESS
Berkeley | Toronto

CONTENTS

PLACE PHOTO OF BABY IN
BIRTHDAY SUIT HERE

....

BABY'S NAME

FAMILY TREE

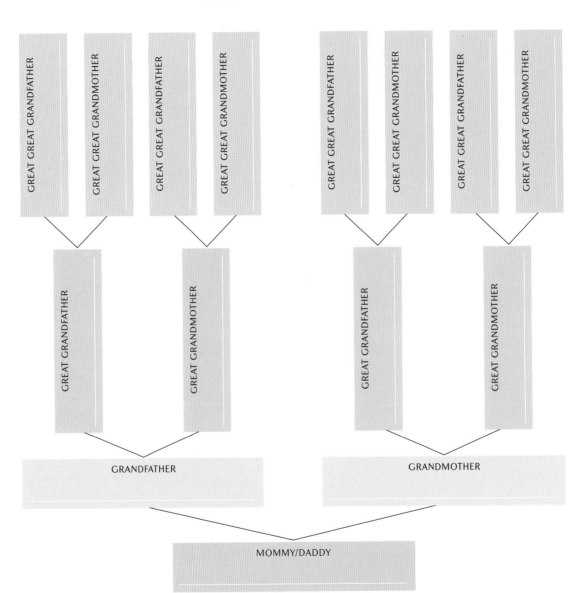

GREAT GREAT GRANDFATHER

GREAT GREAT GRANDMOTHER

GREAT GREAT GRANDFATHER

GREAT GREAT GRANDMOTHER

GREAT GREAT GRANDFATHER

GREAT GREAT GRANDMOTHER

GREAT GREAT GRANDFATHER

GREAT GREAT GRANDMOTHER

GREAT GRANDFATHER

GREAT GRANDMOTHER

GREAT GRANDFATHER

GREAT GRANDMOTHER

GRANDFATHER

GRANDMOTHER

MOMMY/DADDY

FAMILY TREE

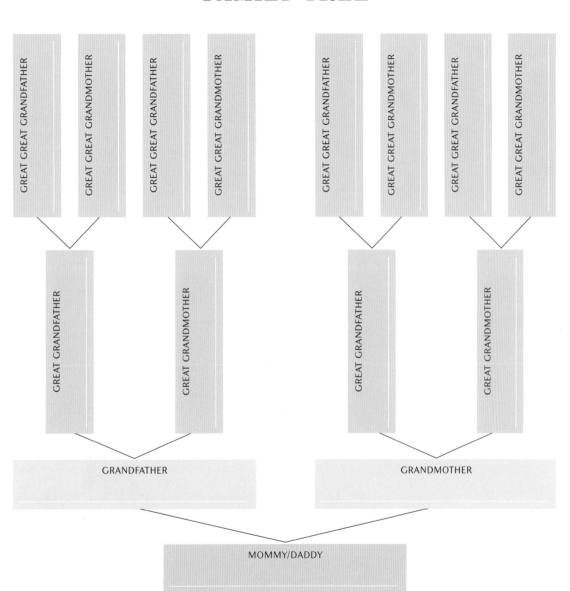

THINKING ABOUT BABY

Nickname(s) before you were born _____

Books we read about raising you _____

_____

Music we listened to while pregnant _____

_____

Foods Mommy craved while pregnant _____

_____

Foods Mommy didn't like while pregnant _____

_____

Our favorite pregnancy memory _____

_____

_____

_____

_____

PLACE PREGNANCY PHOTO HERE

BABY SHOWER

Date _____ Host(s) _____

Who came _____   Guests' comments _____

_____   _____

_____   _____

_____   _____

_____   _____

Gifts _____   _____

_____   _____

_____   _____

_____   _____

PLACE SHOWER INVITATION
OR OTHER MEMENTOS HERE

DOCTOR VISITS

Date _____   The doctor said _____

_____

Date _____   The doctor said _____

_____

Date _____   The doctor said _____

_____

Date _____   The doctor said _____

_____

Date _____   The doctor said _____

_____

Date _____   The doctor said _____

_____

Date _____   The doctor said _____

_____

When we heard your heart beating _____

_____

When Mommy felt you move for the first time _____

_____

Baby's due date _____

Baby is [circle one]   active   not so active

PLACE SONOGRAM PHOTO HERE

THE BIG DAY

Birth date _____   Time _____

Weight _____   Length _____

Where you were born _____

_____

_____

_____

Who delivered you _____

_____

HAIR COLOR
[circle one]

black   red

brown   blond

no hair!

EYE COLOR
[circle one]

blue   gray

brown   hazel

green   black

PLACE NEWBORN PHOTO HERE

MORE ABOUT THE BIG DAY

Labor lasted _____ hours

Who was in the delivery room _____

What the doctor and nurses said _____

_____

What you looked like _____

_____

First visitors to hold you _____

What they said _____

_____

Other visitors _____

_____

In the news that day _____

_____

_____

BABY'S BIRTH STORY

PLACE MEMENTOS FROM BIRTH DAY HERE

NAMING BABY

Your full name is _____

It means _____

_____

We chose your name because _____

_____

Your name was almost _____

_____

BABY'S BIRTH STONE
[circle one]

 JANUARY
GARNET

 FEBRUARY
AMETHYST

 MARCH
AQUAMARINE

 APRIL
DIAMOND

 MAY
EMERALD

 JUNE
PEARL

 JULY
RUBY

AUGUST
PERIDOT

 SEPTEMBER
SAPPHIRE

OCTOBER
OPAL

NOVEMBER
TOPAZ

DECEMBER
TURQUOISE

BABY'S BIRTH SIGN
[circle one]

 ARIES

 TAURUS

 GEMINI

 CANCER

 LEO

 VIRGO

 LIBRA

 SCORPIO

 SAGITTARIUS

 CAPRICORN

 AQUARIUS

 PISCES

BABY'S HANDPRINTS

DATE _____

BABY'S FOOTPRINTS

DATE _____

BABY'S HOMECOMING

Date _____

What you wore home _____

Where the outfit came from _____

PLACE PHOTO OF BABY AT HOME HERE

BABY'S FIRST SLEEPING BUDDY

❏ DOLL

❏ STUFFED ANIMAL

❏ BLANKET

WHERE BABY LIVES

Address _____

Who lives with you _____

_____

What your room looks like _____

_____

Who came to visit _____

_____

Your first night at home was _____

_____

You slept _____

_____

You woke _____

_____

LITTLE THINGS ABOUT BABY

Your eyes look like _____

Your nose looks like _____

Your mouth looks like _____

Your ears look like _____

Birthmarks _____

Your character _____

_____

Other cute little things about baby _____

_____

_____

_____

_____

_____

SIZE OF HANDS [check one]

❏ big!   ❏ not so big

❏ small   ❏ teeny-tiny

SIZE OF FEET [check one]

❏ big!   ❏ not so big

❏ small   ❏ teeny-tiny

FIRST BATH AT HOME

PLACE PHOTO OF BABY'S FIRST BATH HERE

BABY'S FIRST BATH WAS [circle one]

Quiet   Splashy

PLACE BIRTH ANNOUNCEMENT HERE

VISITOR COMMENTS

DATE _____

Meals per day _____   You sleep every _____ hours

Milestones _____

_____

_____

_____

HAPPY TIMES

Games we play _____

_____

_____

BABY'S LIKES & DISLIKES

☆ ☆ ☆ ☆ ☆ _____   ☆ ☆ ☆ ☆ ☆ _____

☆ ☆ ☆ ☆ ☆ _____   ☆ ☆ ☆ ☆ ☆ _____

ABOUT BABY

_____

_____

_____

★ ☆ ☆ ☆ ☆   ★ ★ ☆ ☆ ☆   ★ ★ ★ ☆ ☆   ★ ★ ★ ★ ☆   ★ ★ ★ ★ ★
Baby *really* doesn't like   Baby doesn't like   Baby neither likes nor dislikes   Baby likes   Baby *loves*!

DATE _____

Meals per day _____   You sleep every _____ hours

Milestones _____

_____

_____

Games we play _____

_____

_____

to

to

to

to

BABY'S LIKES & DISLIKES

☆ ☆ ☆ ☆ ☆ _____   ☆ ☆ ☆ ☆ ☆ _____

☆ ☆ ☆ ☆ ☆ _____   ☆ ☆ ☆ ☆ ☆ _____

ABOUT BABY

_____

_____

_____

_____

DATE _____

Meals per day _____   You sleep every _____ hours

Milestones _____

_____

_____

Games we play _____

_____

_____

FUSSY TIMES

to

to

HAPPY TIMES

to

to

BABY'S LIKES & DISLIKES

☆ ☆ ☆ ☆ ☆ _____   ☆ ☆ ☆ ☆ ☆ _____

☆ ☆ ☆ ☆ ☆ _____   ☆ ☆ ☆ ☆ ☆ _____

ABOUT BABY

_____

_____

_____

_____

DATE _____

Meals per day _____   You sleep every _____ hours

Milestones _____

_____

_____

Games we play _____

_____

_____

FUSSY TIMES

to

to

HAPPY TIMES

to

to

BABY'S LIKES & DISLIKES

☆ ☆ ☆ ☆ ☆ _____   ☆ ☆ ☆ ☆ ☆ _____

☆ ☆ ☆ ☆ ☆ _____   ☆ ☆ ☆ ☆ ☆ _____

ABOUT BABY

_____

_____

_____

_____

DATE _____

Meals per day _____   You sleep every _____ hours

Milestones _____

_____

_____

Games we play _____

_____

_____

FUSSY TIMES

HAPPY TIMES

BABY'S LIKES & DISLIKES

☆ ☆ ☆ ☆ ☆ _____   ☆ ☆ ☆ ☆ ☆ _____

☆ ☆ ☆ ☆ ☆ _____   ☆ ☆ ☆ ☆ ☆ _____

ABOUT BABY

_____

_____

_____

_____

DATE _____

Meals per day _____   You sleep every _____ hours

Milestones _____

_____

_____

Games we play _____

_____

_____

BABY'S LIKES & DISLIKES

☆ ☆ ☆ ☆ ☆ _____   ☆ ☆ ☆ ☆ ☆ _____

☆ ☆ ☆ ☆ ☆ _____   ☆ ☆ ☆ ☆ ☆ _____

ABOUT BABY

_____

_____

_____

_____

DATE _____

Meals per day _____   You sleep every _____ hours

Milestones _____

_____

_____

Games we play _____

_____

_____

BABY'S LIKES & DISLIKES

☆☆☆☆☆ _____   ☆☆☆☆☆ _____

☆☆☆☆☆ _____   ☆☆☆☆☆ _____

ABOUT BABY

_____

_____

_____

_____

DATE _____

Meals per day _____   You sleep every _____ hours

Milestones _____

_____

_____

Games we play _____

_____

_____

to

to

to

to

BABY'S LIKES & DISLIKES

☆ ☆ ☆ ☆ ☆ _____   ☆ ☆ ☆ ☆ ☆ _____

☆ ☆ ☆ ☆ ☆ _____   ☆ ☆ ☆ ☆ ☆ _____

ABOUT BABY

_____

_____

_____

_____

DATE _____

Meals per day _____   You sleep every _____ hours

Milestones _____

_____

_____

Games we play _____

_____

_____

to

to

to

to

BABY'S LIKES & DISLIKES

☆ ☆ ☆ ☆ ☆ _____   ☆ ☆ ☆ ☆ ☆ _____

☆ ☆ ☆ ☆ ☆ _____   ☆ ☆ ☆ ☆ ☆ _____

ABOUT BABY

_____

_____

_____

_____

DATE _____

Meals per day _____   You sleep every _____ hours

Milestones _____

_____

_____

Games we play _____

_____

_____

FUSSY TIMES

HAPPY TIMES

BABY'S LIKES & DISLIKES

☆ ☆ ☆ ☆ ☆ _____   ☆ ☆ ☆ ☆ ☆ _____

☆ ☆ ☆ ☆ ☆ _____   ☆ ☆ ☆ ☆ ☆ _____

ABOUT BABY

_____

_____

_____

_____

DATE _____

Meals per day _____   You sleep every _____ hours

Milestones _____

_____

_____

Games we play _____

_____

_____

to

to

to

to

BABY'S LIKES & DISLIKES

☆ ☆ ☆ ☆ ☆ _____   ☆ ☆ ☆ ☆ ☆ _____

☆ ☆ ☆ ☆ ☆ _____   ☆ ☆ ☆ ☆ ☆ _____

ABOUT BABY

_____

_____

_____

_____

DATE _____

Meals per day _____   You sleep every _____ hours

Milestones _____

_____

_____

Games we play _____

_____

_____

BABY'S LIKES & DISLIKES

☆ ☆ ☆ ☆ ☆ _____   ☆ ☆ ☆ ☆ ☆ _____

☆ ☆ ☆ ☆ ☆ _____   ☆ ☆ ☆ ☆ ☆ _____

ABOUT BABY

_____

_____

_____

_____

DATE _____

Meals per day _____   You sleep every _____ hours

Milestones _____

_____

_____

Games we play _____

_____

_____

to

to

to

to

BABY'S LIKES & DISLIKES

☆ ☆ ☆ ☆ ☆ _____   ☆ ☆ ☆ ☆ ☆ _____

☆ ☆ ☆ ☆ ☆ _____   ☆ ☆ ☆ ☆ ☆ _____

ABOUT BABY

_____

_____

_____

_____

DATE _____

Meals per day _____   You sleep every _____ hours

Milestones _____

_____

_____

Games we play _____

_____

_____

to

to

to

to

BABY'S LIKES & DISLIKES

☆ ☆ ☆ ☆ ☆ _____   ☆ ☆ ☆ ☆ ☆ _____

☆ ☆ ☆ ☆ ☆ _____   ☆ ☆ ☆ ☆ ☆ _____

ABOUT BABY

_____

_____

_____

_____

DATE _____

Meals per day _____   You sleep every _____ hours

Milestones _____

_____

_____

Games we play _____

_____

_____

BABY'S LIKES & DISLIKES

☆ ☆ ☆ ☆ ☆ _____   ☆ ☆ ☆ ☆ ☆ _____

☆ ☆ ☆ ☆ ☆ _____   ☆ ☆ ☆ ☆ ☆ _____

ABOUT BABY

_____

_____

_____

_____

DATE _____

Meals per day _____   You sleep every _____ hours

Milestones _____

_____

_____

Games we play _____

_____

_____

FUSSY TIMES

HAPPY TIMES

BABY'S LIKES & DISLIKES

☆ ☆ ☆ ☆ ☆ _____   ☆ ☆ ☆ ☆ ☆ _____

☆ ☆ ☆ ☆ ☆ _____   ☆ ☆ ☆ ☆ ☆ _____

ABOUT BABY

_____

_____

_____

_____

DATE _____

Meals per day _____   You sleep every _____ hours

FUSSY TIMES

Milestones _____

_____

_____

Games we play _____

_____

_____

HAPPY TIMES

BABY'S LIKES & DISLIKES

☆☆☆☆☆ _____   ☆☆☆☆☆ _____

☆☆☆☆☆ _____   ☆☆☆☆☆ _____

ABOUT BABY

_____

_____

_____

_____

_____

DATE _____

Meals per day _____   You sleep every _____ hours

Milestones _____

_____

_____

Games we play _____

_____

_____

to

to

HAPPY TIMES

to

to

BABY'S LIKES & DISLIKES

☆ ☆ ☆ ☆ ☆ _____   ☆ ☆ ☆ ☆ ☆ _____

☆ ☆ ☆ ☆ ☆ _____   ☆ ☆ ☆ ☆ ☆ _____

ABOUT BABY

_____

_____

_____

_____

DATE _____

Meals per day _____   You sleep every _____ hours

Milestones _____

_____

_____

Games we play _____

_____

_____

to

to

to

to

BABY'S LIKES & DISLIKES

☆ ☆ ☆ ☆ ☆ _____   ☆ ☆ ☆ ☆ ☆ _____

☆ ☆ ☆ ☆ ☆ _____   ☆ ☆ ☆ ☆ ☆ _____

ABOUT BABY

_____

_____

_____

_____

DATE _____

Meals per day _____   You sleep every _____ hours

Milestones _____

_____

_____

Games we play _____

_____

_____

to

to

to

to

BABY'S LIKES & DISLIKES

☆ ☆ ☆ ☆ ☆ _____   ☆ ☆ ☆ ☆ ☆ _____

☆ ☆ ☆ ☆ ☆ _____   ☆ ☆ ☆ ☆ ☆ _____

ABOUT BABY

_____

_____

_____

_____

DATE _____

Meals per day _____   You sleep every _____ hours

Milestones _____

_____

_____

Games we play _____

_____

_____

FUSSY TIMES

HAPPY TIMES

BABY'S LIKES & DISLIKES

☆ ☆ ☆ ☆ ☆ _____   ☆ ☆ ☆ ☆ ☆ _____

☆ ☆ ☆ ☆ ☆ _____   ☆ ☆ ☆ ☆ ☆ _____

ABOUT BABY

_____

_____

_____

_____

DATE _____

Meals per day _____   You sleep every _____ hours

Milestones _____

_____

_____

Games we play _____

_____

_____

to

to

to

to

BABY'S LIKES & DISLIKES

☆ ☆ ☆ ☆ ☆ _____   ☆ ☆ ☆ ☆ ☆ _____

☆ ☆ ☆ ☆ ☆ _____   ☆ ☆ ☆ ☆ ☆ _____

ABOUT BABY

_____

_____

_____

_____

DATE _____

Meals per day _____   You sleep every _____ hours

Milestones _____

_____

_____

Games we play _____

_____

_____

BABY'S LIKES & DISLIKES

☆ ☆ ☆ ☆ ☆ _____   ☆ ☆ ☆ ☆ ☆ _____

☆ ☆ ☆ ☆ ☆ _____   ☆ ☆ ☆ ☆ ☆ _____

ABOUT BABY

_____

_____

_____

_____

DATE _____

Meals per day _____   You sleep every _____ hours

Milestones _____

_____

_____

Games we play _____

_____

_____

FUSSY TIMES

HAPPY TIMES

BABY'S LIKES & DISLIKES

☆ ☆ ☆ ☆ ☆ _____   ☆ ☆ ☆ ☆ ☆ _____

☆ ☆ ☆ ☆ ☆ _____   ☆ ☆ ☆ ☆ ☆ _____

ABOUT BABY

_____

_____

_____

_____

DATE _____

Meals per day _____   You sleep every _____ hours

Milestones _____

_____

_____

Games we play _____

_____

_____

BABY'S LIKES & DISLIKES

☆ ☆ ☆ ☆ ☆ _____   ☆ ☆ ☆ ☆ ☆ _____

☆ ☆ ☆ ☆ ☆ _____   ☆ ☆ ☆ ☆ ☆ _____

ABOUT BABY

_____

_____

_____

_____

DATE _____

Meals per day _____   You sleep every _____ hours

Milestones _____

_____

_____

Games we play _____

_____

_____

BABY'S LIKES & DISLIKES

☆ ☆ ☆ ☆ ☆ _____   ☆ ☆ ☆ ☆ ☆ _____

☆ ☆ ☆ ☆ ☆ _____   ☆ ☆ ☆ ☆ ☆ _____

ABOUT BABY

_____

_____

_____

_____

DATE _____

Meals per day _____   You sleep every _____ hours

Milestones _____

_____

_____

Games we play _____

_____

_____

FUSSY TIMES

to

to

HAPPY TIMES

to

to

BABY'S LIKES & DISLIKES

☆ ☆ ☆ ☆ ☆ _____   ☆ ☆ ☆ ☆ ☆ _____

☆ ☆ ☆ ☆ ☆ _____   ☆ ☆ ☆ ☆ ☆ _____

ABOUT BABY

_____

_____

_____

_____

DATE _____

Meals per day _____   You sleep every _____ hours

Milestones _____

_____

_____

Games we play _____

_____

_____

FUSSY TIMES

HAPPY TIMES

BABY'S LIKES & DISLIKES

☆ ☆ ☆ ☆ ☆ _____   ☆ ☆ ☆ ☆ ☆ _____

☆ ☆ ☆ ☆ ☆ _____   ☆ ☆ ☆ ☆ ☆ _____

ABOUT BABY

_____

_____

_____

_____

DATE _____

Meals per day _____   You sleep every _____ hours

Milestones _____

_____

_____

Games we play _____

_____

_____

to

to

to

to

BABY'S LIKES & DISLIKES

☆ ☆ ☆ ☆ ☆ _____   ☆ ☆ ☆ ☆ ☆ _____

☆ ☆ ☆ ☆ ☆ _____   ☆ ☆ ☆ ☆ ☆ _____

ABOUT BABY

_____

_____

_____

_____

DATE _____

Meals per day _____   You sleep every _____ hours

Milestones _____

_____

_____

Games we play _____

_____

_____

to

to

HAPPY TIMES

to

to

BABY'S LIKES & DISLIKES

☆ ☆ ☆ ☆ ☆ _____   ☆ ☆ ☆ ☆ ☆ _____

☆ ☆ ☆ ☆ ☆ _____   ☆ ☆ ☆ ☆ ☆ _____

ABOUT BABY

_____

_____

_____

_____

DATE _____

Meals per day _____   You sleep every _____ hours

Milestones _____

_____

_____

Games we play _____

_____

_____

BABY'S LIKES & DISLIKES

☆ ☆ ☆ ☆ ☆ _____   ☆ ☆ ☆ ☆ ☆ _____

☆ ☆ ☆ ☆ ☆ _____   ☆ ☆ ☆ ☆ ☆ _____

ABOUT BABY

_____

_____

_____

_____

DATE _____

Meals per day _____   You sleep every _____ hours

Milestones _____

_____

_____

Games we play _____

_____

_____

BABY'S LIKES & DISLIKES

☆ ☆ ☆ ☆ ☆ _____   ☆ ☆ ☆ ☆ ☆ _____

☆ ☆ ☆ ☆ ☆ _____   ☆ ☆ ☆ ☆ ☆ _____

ABOUT BABY

_____

_____

_____

_____

DATE _____

Meals per day _____   You sleep every _____ hours

Milestones _____

_____

_____

Games we play _____

_____

_____

FUSSY TIMES

to

HAPPY TIMES

to

BABY'S LIKES & DISLIKES

☆ ☆ ☆ ☆ ☆ _____   ☆ ☆ ☆ ☆ ☆ _____

☆ ☆ ☆ ☆ ☆ _____   ☆ ☆ ☆ ☆ ☆ _____

ABOUT BABY

_____

_____

_____

_____

DATE _____

Meals per day _____   You sleep every _____ hours

Milestones _____

_____

_____

Games we play _____

_____

_____

to

to

to

to

BABY'S LIKES & DISLIKES

☆ ☆ ☆ ☆ ☆ _____   ☆ ☆ ☆ ☆ ☆ _____

☆ ☆ ☆ ☆ ☆ _____   ☆ ☆ ☆ ☆ ☆ _____

ABOUT BABY

_____

_____

_____

_____

DATE _____

Meals per day _____   You sleep every _____ hours

Milestones _____

_____

_____

Games we play _____

_____

_____

HAPPY TIMES

BABY'S LIKES & DISLIKES

☆ ☆ ☆ ☆ ☆ _____   ☆ ☆ ☆ ☆ ☆ _____

☆ ☆ ☆ ☆ ☆ _____   ☆ ☆ ☆ ☆ ☆ _____

ABOUT BABY

_____

_____

_____

_____

DATE _____

Meals per day _____   You sleep every _____ hours

Milestones _____

_____

_____

Games we play _____

_____

_____

FUSSY TIMES

to

HAPPY TIMES

to

. . . .

BABY'S LIKES & DISLIKES

☆ ☆ ☆ ☆ ☆ _____   ☆ ☆ ☆ ☆ ☆ _____

☆ ☆ ☆ ☆ ☆ _____   ☆ ☆ ☆ ☆ ☆ _____

. . . .

ABOUT BABY

_____

_____

_____

_____

DATE _____

Meals per day _____   You sleep every _____ hours

Milestones _____

_____

_____

Games we play _____

_____

_____

to

to

to

to

BABY'S LIKES & DISLIKES

☆ ☆ ☆ ☆ ☆ _____   ☆ ☆ ☆ ☆ ☆ _____

☆ ☆ ☆ ☆ ☆ _____   ☆ ☆ ☆ ☆ ☆ _____

ABOUT BABY

_____

_____

_____

_____

DATE _____

Meals per day _____ You sleep every _____ hours

Milestones _____

_____

_____

Games we play _____

_____

_____

to

to

to

to

BABY'S LIKES & DISLIKES

☆ ☆ ☆ ☆ ☆ _____   ☆ ☆ ☆ ☆ ☆ _____

☆ ☆ ☆ ☆ ☆ _____   ☆ ☆ ☆ ☆ ☆ _____

ABOUT BABY

_____

_____

_____

_____

DATE _____

Meals per day _____   You sleep every _____ hours

Milestones _____

_____

_____

Games we play _____

_____

_____

FUSSY TIMES

to

to

HAPPY TIMES

to

to

BABY'S LIKES & DISLIKES

☆ ☆ ☆ ☆ ☆ _____   ☆ ☆ ☆ ☆ ☆ _____

☆ ☆ ☆ ☆ ☆ _____   ☆ ☆ ☆ ☆ ☆ _____

ABOUT BABY

_____

_____

_____

_____

BABY WEEK TO WEEK

DATE _____

Meals per day _____   You sleep every _____ hours

Milestones _____

_____

_____

Games we play _____

_____

_____

FUSSY TIMES

HAPPY TIMES

BABY'S LIKES & DISLIKES

☆ ☆ ☆ ☆ ☆ _____   ☆ ☆ ☆ ☆ ☆ _____

☆ ☆ ☆ ☆ ☆ _____   ☆ ☆ ☆ ☆ ☆ _____

ABOUT BABY

_____

_____

_____

_____

DATE _____

Meals per day _____   You sleep every _____ hours

Milestones _____

_____

_____

Games we play _____

_____

_____

FUSSY TIMES

to

to

HAPPY TIMES

to

to

BABY'S LIKES & DISLIKES

☆ ☆ ☆ ☆ ☆ _____   ☆ ☆ ☆ ☆ ☆ _____

☆ ☆ ☆ ☆ ☆ _____   ☆ ☆ ☆ ☆ ☆ _____

ABOUT BABY

_____

_____

_____

_____

DATE _____

Meals per day _____   You sleep every _____ hours

Milestones _____

_____

_____

Games we play _____

_____

_____

FUSSY TIMES

HAPPY TIMES

BABY'S LIKES & DISLIKES

☆ ☆ ☆ ☆ ☆ _____   ☆ ☆ ☆ ☆ ☆ _____

☆ ☆ ☆ ☆ ☆ _____   ☆ ☆ ☆ ☆ ☆ _____

ABOUT BABY

_____

_____

_____

_____

DATE _____

Meals per day _____   You sleep every _____ hours

Milestones _____

_____

_____

HAPPY TIMES

Games we play _____

_____

_____

BABY'S LIKES & DISLIKES

☆ ☆ ☆ ☆ ☆ _____   ☆ ☆ ☆ ☆ ☆ _____

☆ ☆ ☆ ☆ ☆ _____   ☆ ☆ ☆ ☆ ☆ _____

ABOUT BABY

_____

_____

_____

_____

DATE _____

Meals per day _____   You sleep every _____ hours

Milestones _____

_____

_____

Games we play _____

_____

_____

FUSSY TIMES

to

to

HAPPY TIMES

to

to

BABY'S LIKES & DISLIKES

☆ ☆ ☆ ☆ ☆ _____   ☆ ☆ ☆ ☆ ☆ _____

☆ ☆ ☆ ☆ ☆ _____   ☆ ☆ ☆ ☆ ☆ _____

ABOUT BABY

_____

_____

_____

_____

BABY WEEK TO WEEK

★

69

DATE _____

Meals per day _____   You sleep every _____ hours

Milestones _____

_____

_____

Games we play _____

_____

_____

BABY'S LIKES & DISLIKES

☆☆☆☆☆ _____   ☆☆☆☆☆ _____

☆☆☆☆☆ _____   ☆☆☆☆☆ _____

ABOUT BABY

_____

_____

_____

_____

DATE _____

Meals per day _____   You sleep every _____ hours

Milestones _____

_____

_____

Games we play _____

_____

_____

HAPPY TIMES

BABY'S LIKES & DISLIKES

☆ ☆ ☆ ☆ ☆ _____   ☆ ☆ ☆ ☆ ☆ _____

☆ ☆ ☆ ☆ ☆ _____   ☆ ☆ ☆ ☆ ☆ _____

ABOUT BABY

_____

_____

_____

_____

DATE _____

Meals per day _____   You sleep every _____ hours

Milestones _____

_____

_____

Games we play _____

_____

_____

BABY'S LIKES & DISLIKES

☆ ☆ ☆ ☆ ☆ _____   ☆ ☆ ☆ ☆ ☆ _____

☆ ☆ ☆ ☆ ☆ _____   ☆ ☆ ☆ ☆ ☆ _____

ABOUT BABY

_____

_____

_____

_____

DATE _____

Meals per day _____   You sleep every _____ hours

Milestones _____

_____

_____

Games we play _____

_____

_____

to

to

to

to

BABY'S LIKES & DISLIKES

☆ ☆ ☆ ☆ ☆ _____   ☆ ☆ ☆ ☆ ☆ _____

☆ ☆ ☆ ☆ ☆ _____   ☆ ☆ ☆ ☆ ☆ _____

ABOUT BABY

_____

_____

_____

_____

DATE _____

Meals per day _____   You sleep every _____ hours

Milestones _____

_____

_____

Games we play _____

_____

_____

to

to

to

to

BABY'S LIKES & DISLIKES

☆ ☆ ☆ ☆ ☆ _____   ☆ ☆ ☆ ☆ ☆ _____

☆ ☆ ☆ ☆ ☆ _____   ☆ ☆ ☆ ☆ ☆ _____

ABOUT BABY

_____

_____

_____

_____

DATE _____

Meals per day _____   You sleep every _____ hours

Milestones _____

_____

_____

Games we play _____

_____

_____

BABY'S LIKES & DISLIKES

☆ ☆ ☆ ☆ ☆ _____   ☆ ☆ ☆ ☆ ☆ _____

☆ ☆ ☆ ☆ ☆ _____   ☆ ☆ ☆ ☆ ☆ _____

ABOUT BABY

_____

_____

_____

_____

DATE _____

Meals per day _____   You sleep every _____ hours

Milestones _____

_____

_____

Games we play _____

_____

_____

FUSSY TIMES

HAPPY TIMES

BABY'S LIKES & DISLIKES

☆ ☆ ☆ ☆ ☆ _____   ☆ ☆ ☆ ☆ ☆ _____

☆ ☆ ☆ ☆ ☆ _____   ☆ ☆ ☆ ☆ ☆ _____

ABOUT BABY

_____

_____

_____

_____

DATE _____

Meals per day _____   You sleep every _____ hours

Milestones _____

_____

_____

Games we play _____

_____

_____

FUSSY TIMES

HAPPY TIMES

BABY'S LIKES & DISLIKES

☆ ☆ ☆ ☆ ☆ _____   ☆ ☆ ☆ ☆ ☆ _____

☆ ☆ ☆ ☆ ☆ _____   ☆ ☆ ☆ ☆ ☆ _____

ABOUT BABY

_____

_____

_____

_____

FIRST PET

What you thought about _____
                              [pet's name]

_____

_____

_____

What _____ thought about you _____
          [pet's name]

_____

_____

_____

_____

_____

_____

PLACE PHOTO OF PET AND BABY TOGETHER HERE

FIRST TEETH

DATE EACH TOOTH APPEARED

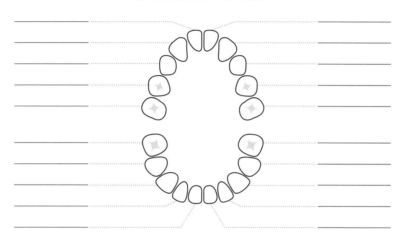

How we handled teething

Your favorite way to relieve teething aches

PLACE MESSY FACE PHOTO HERE

BON APPÉTIT!

When you started eating solid foods _____

Favorite solid foods _____

_____

_____

When you started chewing foods _____

Favorite harder foods _____

_____

_____

Foods you didn't like _____

_____

_____

_____

FIRSTS & FAVORITES

★

83

TALK TO ME, BABY

How we communicated before you could talk _____

_____

_____

_____

_____

First word _____

Who heard it _____

Where _____

Other early words _____

_____

_____

_____

PLACE PHOTO OF FIRST HAIRCUT HERE

FIRST HAIRCUT

Date of your first haircut

POCKET FOR LOCK OF BABY'S HAIR

ON THE MOVE

When you crawled for the first time _____

_____

_____

When you stood for the first time _____

_____

_____

When you walked for the first time _____

_____

_____

Who saw it _____

_____

_____

PLACE PHOTO OF BABY'S EARLY STEPS HERE

SING IT, BABY!

BABY IS A

❏ ROCKER ❏ COUNTRY STAR

  ❏ CLASSICAL ENTHUSIAST ❏ FUTURE RAPPER

❏ POP PRINCE(SS)

When you first started dancing

Favorite song

When you first started singing

FAVORITE DANCE MOVE
[circle one]

bouncing up and down

spinning around

swaying from side to side

all of the above

FAVORITE BOOKS

MOST-READ BOOK

Title ....

Author/Illustrator ....

Notes ....

HUMOROUS BOOK

Title ....

Author/Illustrator ....

Notes ....

BEDTIME BOOK

Title ....

Author/Illustrator ....

Notes ....

WAKE-UP BOOK

Title ....

Author/Illustrator ....

Notes ....

OTHER FAVORITES

Title ....

Author/Illustrator ....

Notes ....

Title ....

Author/Illustrator ....

Notes ....

Date _____

Where we went _____

How we got there _____

Who came with us _____

What we did _____

_____

_____

How you liked it _____

_____

_____

_____

_____

_____

PLACE PHOTO FROM BABY'S FIRST TRIP HERE

FAVORITE TOY

Your favorite toy was a _____ named _____

You received your favorite toy from _____

_____

How you liked to play together _____

_____

_____

_____

Adventures _____ has been on _____
                     [name of toy]

_____

_____

_____

_____

_____

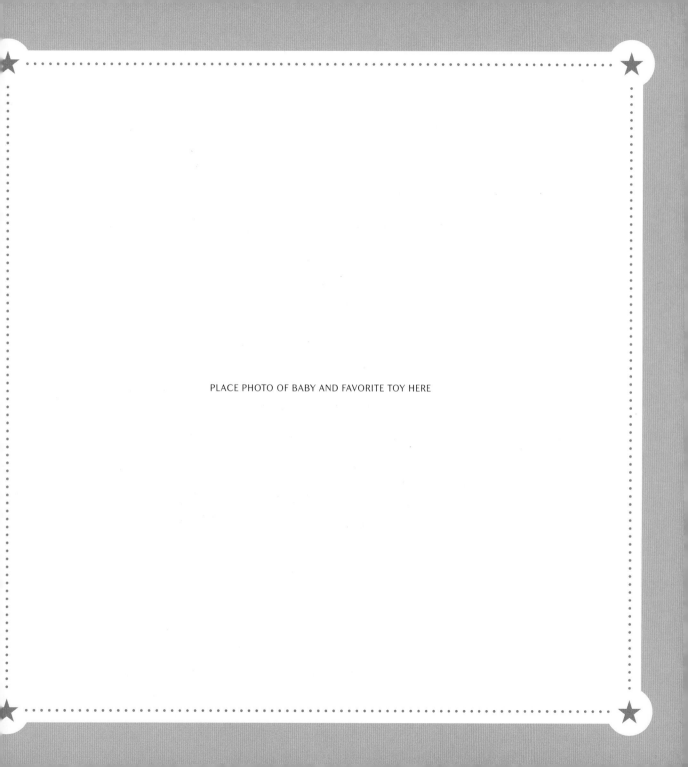

PLACE PHOTO OF BABY AND FAVORITE TOY HERE

FAVORITE ANIMALS

BABY LIKES
[circle favorites]

cows   dogs   lizards   pigs   monkeys   lions

dinosaurs   cats   bugs   fish   birds   chipmunks

sharks   chickens   sheep   tigers   snakes   bunnies

bears   turtles   elephants   horses   other _____

Favorite animal sounds _____

_____

PLACE PHOTO OF BABY WITH FAVORITE ANIMAL HERE

FIRST FRIEND

Name of your friend _____

Where you met _____

What you liked to do together _____

_____

_____

PLACE PHOTO OF BABY WITH FIRST FRIEND HERE

I AM ONE YEAR OLD TODAY!

How we celebrated _____

_____

_____

Guest list _____

_____

_____

_____

_____

Gifts _____

_____

_____

_____

Games we played _____

_____

_____

_____

Kind of cake and what it looked like _____

_____

_____

_____

PLACE PHOTO OF BABY'S FIRST BIRTHDAY HERE

NEW BABIES GROW SO FAST!

LENGTH _____ inches

WEIGHT _____ pounds

DATE _____

LENGTH _____ inches

WEIGHT _____ pounds

DATE _____

LENGTH _____ inches

WEIGHT _____ pounds

DATE _____

LENGTH _____ inches

WEIGHT _____ pounds

DATE _____

LENGTH _____ inches

WEIGHT _____ pounds

DATE _____

LENGTH _____ inches

WEIGHT _____ pounds

DATE _____

LENGTH _____ inches

WEIGHT _____ pounds

DATE _____

LENGTH _____ inches

WEIGHT _____ pounds

DATE _____

Ten Speed Press
Box 7123
Berkeley, California 94707
www.tenspeed.com

Distributed in Australia by Simon and Schuster Australia, in Canada by Ten Speed Press Canada, in New Zealand by Southern Publishers Group, in South Africa by Real Books, and in the United Kingdom and Europe by Publishers Group UK.

Design by Katy Brown and Betsy Stromberg

ISBN 13: 978-1-58008-933-3
ISBN 10: 1-58008-933-X

Printed in China

1 2 3 4 5 6 7 8 9 10 – 12 11 10 09 08